Sara Swan Miller

Horses and Rhinos

What They Have in Common

Franklin Watts - A Division of Grolier Publishing
New York • London • Hong Kong • Sydney • Danbury, Connecticut

For my sister Emily,
A real horse lover

Photographs ©: Animals Animals: 41 (Trevor Barrett), 31 (Robert Maier); Peter Arnold Inc.:
27 (Peter Arnold), 39 (Lionel Atwill), 13 (Fred Bruemmer), 43 (William Campbell), 5 bottom
right (Doug Cheeseman), 32, 33 (Foto Sorrel), 29 (M. Gunther/BIOS), 19, 25 (Gerard Lacz),
6 top (Fritz Prenzel), 35 (Kevin Schafer); Photo Researchers: 21 (Mark D. Phillips); Tony Stone
Images: 17 (Daniel J. Cox), 40 (Bruce Hands), 15 (Kim Heacox), 1 (Mitch Reardon), cover
(Thomas Zimmermann); Visuals Unlimited: 22, 23 (Ken Lucas), 6 bottom (Joe McDonald),
37 (John C. Muegge), 5 top left (Mark Newman), 42 (Jo Prater); Wildlife Collection: 5 bottom
left, 7 (Martin Harvey), 5 top right (Swenson).

Illustrations by Jose Gonzales and Steve Savage

Visit Franklin Watts on the Internet at:
http://publishing.grolier.com

Library of Congress Cataloging-in-Publication Data

Miller, Sara Swan.
Horses and rhinos: what they have in common / Sara Swan Miller.
    p. cm. — (Animals in order)
  Includes bibliographical references and index.
  Summary: Describes members of the order of animals that have hooves with an odd number
of toes, including horses, rhinoceroses, tapirs, asses, and zebras.
    ISBN 0-531-11586-0 (lib. bdg.)   0-531-16401-2 (pbk.)
    1. Perissodactyla—Juvenile literature. [1. Ungulates] I. Title. II. Series.
  QL737.U6M56 1999
  599.66–dc21   98-8205
                                                                 CIP
                                                                AC

Contents

Horses, Rhinos, Tapirs, and Zebras: What Do They Share?

It's hard to believe that horses, rhinoceroses (rhinos for short), tapirs, and zebras all belong to the same group of animals. Maybe you can see how a horse and a zebra are similar. But how is a sleek, fast-running horse similar to a huge, big-bellied rhino? And how is a hard-galloping, many-striped zebra related to a long-nosed, piglike tapir?

Even though these animals look very different, they share many common characteristics. On the next page you will see a zebra, a horse, a rhino, and a tapir. Can you tell how they are similar?

Wild mustang

Baird's tapir

Black rhinoceros

Burchell's zebra

Traits of the Perissodactyls: Odd-toed Hoofed Animals

Horses, rhinos, tapirs, and zebras all have the same kind of feet—hooves with an odd number of toes. Scientists call the animals in this group *perissodactyls* (puhr-ISS-uh-DAK-tils), which means "odd-toed." Other hoofed animals, such as deer and antelope, have an even number of toes.

Perissodactyls run high on their toes, and they are fast. Horses, zebras, and donkeys run the fastest. Their long legs help them cover a lot of ground with each stride. Even slow-looking rhinos can move quickly.

An Arabian horse runs on one toe.

A black rhino runs on three toes.

Horses, zebras, and donkeys run on one toe. If your hand were a hoof, that toe would be your middle finger. Tapirs and rhinos put most of their weight on their middle toes. Tapirs have five toes on their front hooves and three toes on their back hooves. Rhinos have three toes on all four hooves.

The teeth of perissodactyls are perfect for eating grass and other plants. Most have front teeth that are suited for biting off plant material. Their back teeth fit closely together and are good for chewing plants. Because grasses and other plants are hard to digest, perissodactyls depend on tiny *bacteria* inside their gut to break down the plants.

The Order of Living Things

A tiger has more in common with a house cat than with a daisy. A true bug is more like a butterfly than a jellyfish. Scientists arrange living things into groups based on how they look and how they act. A tiger and a house cat belong to the same group, but a daisy belongs to a different group.

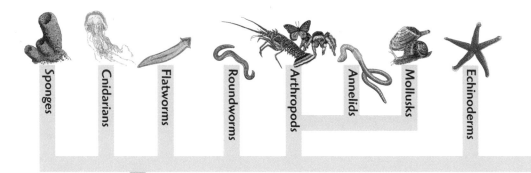

All living things can be placed in one of five groups called *kingdoms*: the plant kingdom, the animal kingdom, the fungus kingdom, the moneran kingdom, or the protist kingdom. You can probably name many of the creatures in the plant and animal kingdoms. The fungus kingdom includes mushrooms, yeasts, and molds. The moneran and protist kingdoms contain thousands of living things that are too small to see without a microscope.

8

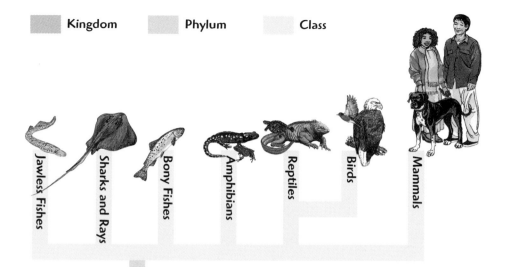

Kingdom   Phylum   Class

Jawless Fishes

Sharks and Rays

Bony Fishes

Amphibians

Reptiles

Birds

Mammals

Chordates

Because there are millions and millions of living things on Earth, some of the members of one kingdom may not seem all that similar. The animal kingdom includes creatures as different as tarantulas and trout, jellyfish and jaguars, salamanders and sparrows, elephants and earthworms.

To show that an elephant is more like a jaguar than an earthworm, scientists further separate the creatures in each kingdom into more specific groups. The animal kingdom can be divided into nine *phyla*. Humans belong to the chordate phylum. Almost all chordates have a backbone.

Each phylum can be subdivided into many *classes*. Humans, mice, and elephants all belong to the *mammal* class. Each class can be further divided into *orders*; orders into *families*, families into *genera*, and genera into *species*. All the members of a species are very similar.

How Perissodactyls Fit In

You can probably guess that the perissodactyls belong to the animal kingdom. They have much more in common with bees and bats than with maple trees and morning glories.

Perissodactyls belong to the chordate phylum. Almost all chordates have a backbone and a skeleton. Can you think of other chordates? Examples include lions, mice, snakes, birds, fish, and whales.

The chordate phylum can be divided into several classes. Perissodactyls belong to the mammal class. Mice, whales, dogs, cats, and humans are all mammals.

There are seventeen different orders of mammals. The perissodactyls make up one of the four orders of mammals with hooves, which scientists call *ungulates*. Deer, antelope, giraffes, cows, and elephants are other kinds of ungulates. For millions of years, there were more perissodactyls on Earth than any other kind of ungulates. But over time, the hoofed animals with an even number of toes were more successful at finding food.

Today, only three families of perissodactyls are left—horses and zebras, rhinos, and tapirs. Each family has many different genera and species. They live in deserts, grasslands, and forest *habitats*, mostly in the warmer parts of the world. In this book, you will learn more about some of the perissodactyls.

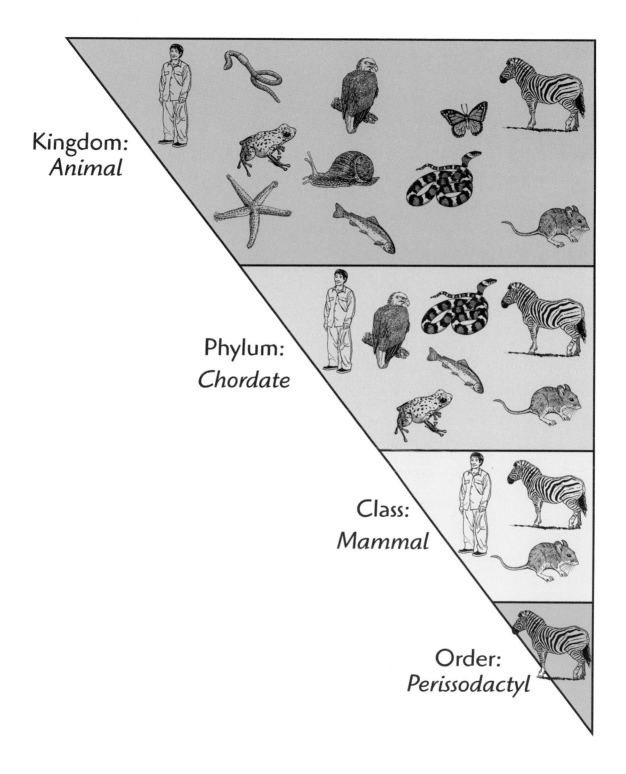

Kingdom:
Animal

Phylum:
Chordate

Class:
Mammal

Order:
Perissodactyl

Zebras

FAMILY: Equidae
EXAMPLE: Grevy's zebra
GENUS AND SPECIES: *Equus grevyi*
SIZE: 54 to 60 inches (137 to 152 cm) high at
the shoulder

Zebras have fascinated people for thousands of years. The ancient Romans called them "tiger horses" and paraded them through the streets for everyone to see. You can tell a Grevy's zebra from other species of zebras because its stripes are thin and very close together.

The stripes on a zebra are like fingerprints on people. No two zebras have the exact same pattern of stripes, so it's easy to identify them. Have you ever wondered whether zebras are black with white stripes or white with black stripes? To find out, you would have to shave one. If you did, you'd see that their skin is black. This means that they are black with white stripes!

How does having stripes help zebras? No one knows for sure. Maybe the different patterns make it easier for them to tell each other apart. Or maybe the stripes help them hide in the tall grasses of the African plains. When zebras run, the stripes might confuse a lion, making it difficult for the hungry *predator* to chase a single zebra. Some people think a zebra's stripes may protect it from biting flies. Flies can only see large patches of black and white. Since they can't see a zebra's narrow stripes, flies usually leave zebras alone.

Most zebras travel in large *herds*, but Grevy's zebras don't always stay together. Sometimes one of these animals may even wander about on its own.

Zebras

FAMILY: Equidae
COMMON EXAMPLE: Burchell's zebra
GENUS AND SPECIES: *Equus burchelli*
SIZE: 54 inches (137 cm) high at the shoulder

On a wide African plain, a huge herd of zebras moves slowly, grazing on grasses. Other animals, such as wildebeest and antelope, travel with them. Even though this herd looks big and disorganized, the zebras actually stay together in family groups. In each family, the *stallion* protects his *mares* and *foals*. With ears pointed forward, he is always alert.

Suddenly, one stallion sees a lion creeping toward the herd. He barks a warning and stamps his hooves. The mares and foals gallop away as fast as they can, and the stallion chases after them. When the lion is right on the stallion's heels, he kicks the lion in the face with his hard, sharp hooves. Then he speeds away, leaving the lion shaking its aching head. No zebra dinner for the lion this time!

In the dry season, herds of Burchell's zebras roam the plains, searching for patches of grass. But when the rains come and new grass sprouts, the zebras stay in one place. This is when baby zebras are born. Newborn zebras have to learn to stand right away so that lions and hyenas won't eat them. Only an hour after they are born, baby zebras are already skipping about, ready to race away at the first sign of danger.

14

Rhinoceroses

FAMILY: Rhinocerotidae
EXAMPLE: Black rhinoceros
GENUS AND SPECIES: *Diceros bicornis*
SIZE: 56 to 60 inches (142 to 152 cm) high at
the shoulder

You might expect black rhinos to be black, but their thick skin is actually a bluish-gray color. The only time these rhinos look black is when they are covered with black mud. They like to live near water holes so they can cool off by rolling in the mud. The mud protects them from the hot midday sun and keeps flies from biting.

Black rhinos usually live alone in brushy places, browsing on trees and shrubs. They wrap their pointed upper lip around twigs and pull the plants into their mouths. These giant beasts have two horns on their nose. The horns are not made of bone, like those of other animals. Instead, the black rhino's horns are made of *keratin*, the material that makes up human hair and fingernails.

Male black rhinos mark their territories with piles of dung. They scatter their droppings with their hind legs and flatten them with their front horn. The pile may be more than 6 feet (2 m) across. The droppings tell other males, "Go away! You're trespassing!" But to females they mean, "I'm here! Come find me!"

About the only time you'll see black rhinos together is when a mother is traveling with her calf. Stay away! If an enemy threatens her calf, a mother rhino will charge without warning. Rhinos run faster than you might think—up to 30 miles (48 km) an hour. They are very strong, too. One angry rhino charged a train and knocked it off the tracks!

Rhinoceroses

FAMILY: Rhinocerotidae

EXAMPLE: White rhinoceros

GENUS AND SPECIES: *Ceratotherium simum*

SIZE: 60 to 84 inches (152 to 213 cm) high at
the shoulder

White rhinos aren't white any more than black rhinos are black. White rhinos are the same bluish-gray color as black rhinos, and they also have two horns. So how can you tell these two kinds of rhinos apart? The white rhino has a flat lip and a wide, square mouth that is good for biting off grass. Its name comes from an Afrikaans (Dutch South African) word meaning "wide," which turned into "white."

White rhinos travel together in herds of about a dozen animals. They wander around the grasslands with their heads low, grazing quietly. From dusk to dawn, they feed together. But when the hot African sun rises, they head for the shade or the cooling mud of a water hole.

With their huge size, tough skin, and sharp horns, adult rhinos have no enemies—except humans. For many years, people have hunted rhinos for their horns. At one time, some people living in the Middle East used rhino horns to make fancy dagger handles. Other people ground the horns to make medicines. Sadly, rhinos are now in danger of becoming *extinct*. Without our protection, these giant animals may not survive.

Asses

FAMILY: Equidae
EXAMPLE: Somali ass
GENUS AND SPECIES: *Equus asinus*
SIZE: 48 inches (122 cm) high at the shoulder

On the dry African desert, a newborn Somali ass struggles to its feet. Its mother licks the young animal dry as it stands wobbling in the sun. With its soft gray coat and pretty striped "stockings," the newborn looks just like its mother, only smaller.

This baby ass must get used to standing right away. Lions and hyenas are hiding nearby, hoping for a tasty dinner. The mother ass stands guard, with her long ears pointed forward. If danger threatens, she's ready to drive off an attacker with her strong teeth and sharp hooves.

But before long, the foal is ready to run with the herd. It soon learns to look and listen for danger. If an enemy attacks, the young ass can race away at speeds of up to 40 miles (64 km) an hour. It also learns how to climb steep hills and hide among the broken rocks, safe from danger.

Somali asses are well suited to desert life. Their gray coats blend with the sand, hiding them from predators. They can wander for days without drinking water, living on tough desert grasses and stunted, thorny bushes. Although Somali asses are tough enough to survive the harsh desert climate, they, too are *endangered*. Over the years, people have hunted them as food. Because Somali asses now compete for food and water with farm animals, it may be only a matter of time before the last Somali ass dies out.

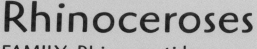

Rhinoceroses

FAMILY: Rhinocerotidae
COMMON EXAMPLE: Indian rhinoceros
GENUS AND SPECIES: *Rhinoceros unicornis*
SIZE: 66 inches (168 cm) high at the shoulder

An Indian rhino and its baby crash slowly through the tall, thick grass. A mynah bird rides peacefully on the mother's back, pecking at insects on her hide. Suddenly the mynah flies up, squawking loudly. Danger!

The mother rhino lifts her head and sniffs deeply. Tiger! Without another thought, she charges blindly. The tiger races away, and the baby rhino is safe. The mother trots back to her baby, rubs it with her nose, and comforts it with soft, mewing sounds.

Like all mother rhinos, this female watches out for her baby until the young rhino is large enough to defend itself. When the rhino grows up, it will have the same tough protective skin as its mother. No tiger will be able to hurt it then!

Adult Indian rhinos spend most of their time alone. They roam through thickets and

22

grasslands, munching grasses as they go. In the heat of the day, they cool off in the river and eat the water plants that grow there.

Indian rhinos live a peaceful life, except at mating time. Then the males fight fiercely over the females, slashing at each other with their horns. Sometimes these battles go on until one rhino dies!

Rhinoceroses

FAMILY: Rhinocerotidae
EXAMPLE: Sumatran rhinoceros
GENUS AND SPECIES: *Dicerorhinus sumatrensis*
SIZE: 54 inches (137 cm) high at the shoulder

Deep in a dense rain forest, a Sumatran rhino pushes its way slowly through the underbrush. It stops often to munch on leafy twigs and shrubs in its path. Is there a tasty piece of fruit at the top of that small tree? To find out, the rhino simply pushes the tree down. Mmm! The fruit is delicious!

Sumatran rhinos are small and hairy. Their thickly folded skin is covered with stiff, reddish-brown hair. In zoos, their coats may be shaggy. Like other rhinos, Sumatran rhinos can't see very well. Their eyesight is so poor that they may run into a tree or bush by mistake. But they have good hearing and an excellent sense of smell. Rhinos walk with their noses turned into the wind, checking the air for danger. When they smell trouble, they charge blindly and without warning. If they accidentally charge in the wrong direction, they turn around right away and charge again.

Because the rain forests are being destroyed and because people have hunted them for their horns for many years, these rhinos are now very rare. Only about 500 Sumatran rhinos are left in the wild. Today, they are protected in nature preserves, but it may be too late to save them from extinction.

24

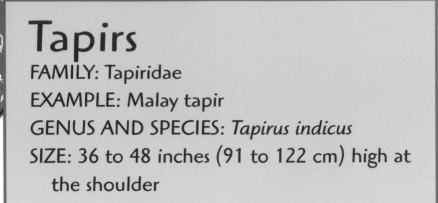

Tapirs

FAMILY: Tapiridae
EXAMPLE: Malay tapir
GENUS AND SPECIES: *Tapirus indicus*
SIZE: 36 to 48 inches (91 to 122 cm) high at
    the shoulder

A Malay tapir jogs down a well-worn path in a rain forest. It looks like a pig wearing a blanket—a pig with a long, strange nose. Every so often the tapir stops and raises its trunk-like nose, sniffing for danger. All clear! The tapir wraps its short trunk around a branch, strips off the leaves, and shoves them into its mouth. Then it trots on toward its water hole.

Malay tapirs are well suited to life in rain forests. Their bodies are compact and streamlined, perfect for pushing through the dense undergrowth. Their black and white patches break up the outline of their body, making it hard for predators to recognize them. Their short trunk lets them reach up to grab leaves and fruit.

Tapirs are excellent swimmers. If a tiger comes too close, a tapir can slide down a steep riverbank, slip into the water, and swim away swiftly. Or it can dive underwater and stay there until the tiger gives up.

Tapirs can often escape from tigers, but they aren't safe from people. They are hunted for food and for their thick skin, which can be made into leather. Because tapirs use the same trails again

and again, it is easy for people to track them. People are also destroying their forest homes. Sadly, the Malay tapir, the rarest of all tapirs, is now endangered.

Horses

FAMILY: Equidae

EXAMPLE: Przewalski's horse

GENUS AND SPECIES: *Equus przewalskii*

SIZE: 48 to 54 inches (122 to 137 cm) high at
    the shoulder

Przewalski's horse is short and stocky, with a smooth grayish-brown coat and a black streak along its back. While most horses have *forelocks*—bunches of hair growing from the front of their heads—Przewalski's horses do not. These wild horses have never been tamed, but they were hunted for thousands of years. Cave paintings in southern France show that ancient humans hunted them for food.

At one time, Przewalski's horses roamed freely all over Europe and Asia. As these hardy horses traveled in herds over the plains, they munched on short, dry grasses. Now the only Przewalski's horses left on Earth live in zoos. No one has seen one of these horses in the wild for more than 30 years. The last one was seen in the Gobi Desert in 1968.

Many people are now interested in protecting Przewalski's horses. One group has set up a special wildlife preserve for them. Here, a small herd is safe from enemies. When they get used to living in the wild again, some may be released into their natural habitat. Maybe these wild horses can roam free once more.

29

Asses

FAMILY: Equidae
EXAMPLE: Asiatic ass
GENUS AND SPECIES: *Equus hemonius*
SIZE: 48 inches (122 cm) high at the shoulder

On a windy, sun-scorched plain in India, a herd of Asiatic asses huddles together with their heads lowered. They shelter one another from the strong wind and the stinging sand that whips across the dry desert. When the wind dies down, the animals continue their hunt for tough grasses growing out of the sand. These grasses appear suddenly after rainstorms and wither quickly.

In the coolness of the early morning and evening, Asiatic asses travel far and wide in search of food. Life in the desert is hard, but these asses can survive because they will eat almost any kind of plant—even a thornbush. And they can live for a long time without water. Traveling in herds helps the asses avoid enemies, such as wolves. As they graze, they turn their large ears constantly and often sniff the air. They know the sounds and smells of danger. When Asiatic asses sense a predator, they race away on their tough hooves. They can run up to 40 miles (64 km) an hour!

Great herds of wild asses once roamed the Asian plains. But now they are nearly all gone. For years they have been hunted for their flesh and hides. More recently, they have had to compete with grazing farm animals for food and water.

30

Horses

FAMILY: Equidae
COMMON EXAMPLE: Camargue horse
GENUS AND SPECIES: *Equus caballus*
SIZE: 56 inches (142 cm) high at the shoulder

Have you ever heard of a region of France called Camargue? The saltwater marshes in this area are the home of Camargue horses. As they splash through the marshes' shallow waters, their long shaggy manes and flowing tails seem to float behind them in the brisk wind. Brown foals run beside their creamy-white mothers. When the horses reach a stand of marsh grass, they stop, lower their large heads, and tug at the tough grass. Then they wander on, pausing now and then to sip the salty water.

Camargue horses are a very old type of horse. They were originally *bred* to herd the famous Camargue bulls. These horses are fast and agile—they can twist and turn quickly to round up the bulls.

Herds of Camargue horses have roamed wild in the Camargue region of southern

France for more than 1,000 years. Recently, this area has been made into a nature preserve to protect them. The horses share the preserve with black bulls, sheep, seabirds, bustards, and flamingos. From time to time, local farmers round up the horses to count and brand them. The ranchers keep some of the horses to work with their bulls, but most are set free to roam wild in the salty marshes and along the sandy beaches.

Tapirs

FAMILY: Tapiridae
EXAMPLE: Baird's tapir
GENUS AND SPECIES: *Tapirella bairdii*
SIZE: 24 to 48 inches (61 to 122 cm) high at
the shoulder

A young Baird's tapir trots along behind its mother as she pushes her way through the dense undergrowth. The baby looks like a brown watermelon on legs. The stripes and patterns on its back help the young tapir blend in with the jungle floor. If the tapir is quiet, a hungry predator may not spot it.

The mother tapir sniffs the air with her trunk and swivels her ears to catch the slightest sound of danger. She has an excellent sense of smell and a good sense of hearing, but she can't see very well with her tiny eyes.

Baird's tapirs have many ways to escape their enemies. They can run fast, slide down riverbanks, dive and hide underwater for a long time, or swim away quickly. They are good climbers, too. Captive tapirs have been known to climb the fence around their pen and race off to freedom. If a tapir can escape its enemies, it may live up to 30 years!

But one enemy spells real trouble for tapirs—people. Each year, farmers destroy more and more of the animals' rain forest homes to grow crops or raise cattle. Hunters also kill tapirs for food and sport.

Many tapirs die of diseases they catch from farm animals, such as horses. For all these reasons, Baird's tapirs are endangered animals.

Many people are worried about tapirs. They are working to save the tapirs' habitat and protect them from hunters. Tapirs may yet make a comeback.

Horses

FAMILY: Equidae
COMMON EXAMPLE: Wild mustang
GENUS AND SPECIES: *Equus caballus*
SIZE: 54 inches (137 cm) high at the shoulder

With their ears flattened back and their huge teeth flashing, two wild mustang stallions fight over a group of mares. Kicking and biting, the horses arch their necks and rear against each other. Finally, one of the males gives up. He gallops away, leaving the winner to claim the mares.

Wild mustangs travel together in bands of up to twenty horses. While the mares and foals munch on grasses, the stallion stands guard. Because a horse's eyes are on the sides of its head, the stallion can see in every direction without moving his head. He can detect the slightest sound by swiveling his ears back and forward. Even if a mountain lion attacks, the stallion will put up a good fight. The flailing hooves of a wild mustang often discourage predators.

Wild mustangs are closely related to the horses brought to the Americas hundreds of years ago by Spanish explorers and European settlers. That is why they have the same genus and species names as the Camargue horses that live in France today. When the European horses escaped from their corrals, they became *feral* animals—wild animals that were once tame. The horses often formed wild herds and ran free on the Western plains.

About 100 years ago, 2 million feral mustangs ran wild in the western United States. Today only about 30,000 of these animals are left. Because their original *territory* is now being used to grow crops and raise cattle, there isn't much space left for wild mustangs. Small herds of these beautiful horses continue to run free on special wildlife preserves where they are protected.

Burros

FAMILY: Equidae
COMMON EXAMPLE: Wild burro
GENUS AND SPECIES: *Equus asinus*
SIZE: 48 inches (122 cm) high at the shoulder

A small herd of wild burros picks its way down a rocky slope. The burros pause every now and then to tug at tufts of tough grass or nibble on thorny plants sprouting among the rocks. The slope gets steeper, but that doesn't stop the burros. They keep making their way carefully down until they reach the valley floor. Finally, a water hole! The thirsty burros drink greedily. It has been days since they have had a drink.

These rugged little burros are well suited to the harsh, dry lands where they live. Like their close relatives the Somali asses, wild burros can survive on very little food and even less water. They can also climb up and down steep, rocky hills without losing their footing.

Like wild mustangs, wild burros are feral animals. They are closely related to the donkeys and asses that carried the packs of early American gold prospectors over rough, uneven ground. That is why they have the same genus and species names as the Somali asses that live in Africa today. The gold prospectors valued the burros because they are hardy, strong, and, above all, sure-footed. After the gold rush, many of the burros ran off and formed wild herds.

38

Everyone knows the loud braying sound that a burro makes—
"hee-haw! hee-haw!" Each burro has its own special call, so burros
can recognize one another by their braying sounds. Burros may not
be very musical, but some people call them "Rocky Mountain
canaries."

Perissodactyls and People

Thousands of years ago, people realized that they could tame wild horses and asses and put them to work. They used them to pull and carry heavy loads and to travel quickly from place to place. They developed hundreds of different *breeds* to meet their needs—race-horses, draft horses, riding horses, and horses for herding cattle. They even bred burros with horses to create strong, sure-footed mules.

Five horses pull the plow of an Amish farmer.

As long as people could find a use for some perissodactyls, these animals increased in number. But others have not been so lucky. All perissodactyls, except for domestic horses and burros, are now endangered or may soon become endangered. They are close to extinction because our actions have threatened their populations and their habitats.

The few Przewalski's horses that still survive live in zoos. People could not tame these horses, so they hunted them for food. Humans also hunted wild mustangs, burros, and the wild asses of Africa and Asia for their meat and hides. Now these animals are nearly gone. Will rhinos survive? People have long hunted these animals for their horns. In just 30 years, 97 percent of the world's rhinos have disappeared. People found that tapirs were easy to hunt. They followed their well-worn paths through the jungle and killed the tapirs for

Rhino horns

their meat and their tough hides. Now tapirs are endangered. The beautiful patterns of zebras' coats made them a target for hunters. Before hunting zebras became illegal in Kenya, a country in east Africa, people could buy a zebra coat for $600 or a handbag for $85. People hunted these animals almost to the point of extinction.

When people turn deserts and plains into farms or grazing land for cattle, animals such as wild horses, wild asses, rhinos, and zebras are crowded out. When humans clear rain forests to make room for crops or livestock, tapirs are crammed into ever-smaller areas, and their numbers shrink. People are taking over many of the wild areas in the world, and wild animals are paying the price.

What can be done to save the perissodactyls from extinction? In recent years, people around the world have become concerned. Finally, we have started to look for ways to protect these animals. In many places, laws now protect animals such as rhinos, tapirs, and

A park ranger cares for two rhinos.

zebras from hunters. These laws are beginning to make a difference. But there are always *poachers*—people who will break the law if they think they can make money. Rangers are on the lookout for these poachers, but they can't catch them all.

Habitat protection is another way to save perissodactyls from extinction. People are now setting up nature preserves around the world where endangered animals can live safely and begin to make a comeback.

Despite these efforts, some species are now so rare that we

This army officer (left) is arresting two poachers in Tanzania, Africa.

must do more than simply protect them in the wild. To save these animals, zoos have set up breeding programs. When protected herds of Przewalski's horses and wild asses grow large enough, scientists hope to release some of the animals into their natural habitats. With so many people working to protect them, maybe horses, rhinos, tapirs, and zebras will roam wild and free for many more centuries.

Words to Know

bacteria—tiny creatures that are members of the moneran kingdom.

bred (verb, past tense of **breed**)—chose specific animals to mate and have young in order to develop an animal with a particular appearance or behavior.

breed (noun)—a group of animals with physical traits and behaviors chosen by humans. A breeder picks specific animals to mate and have young based on their appearance and behavior.

class—a group of creatures within a phylum that share certain characteristics.

endangered—in danger of extinction.

extinct—no longer in existence.

family—a group of creatures within an order that share certain characteristics.

feral—an animal that was once domesticated, but escaped and is now wild.

foal—a young horse, ass, or zebra.

forelock—a bunch of hair that grows from the front of a horse's head.

genus (plural **genera**)—a group of creatures within a family that share certain characteristics.

habitat—the natural environment of an animal or plant.

herd—a group of animals that travel and eat together.

keratin—the material that makes up hair and fingernails.

kingdom—the largest group of biological classification.

mammal—an animal with a backbone that has fur and feeds its young with mother's milk.

mare—a female horse, ass, or zebra.

order—a group of creatures within a class that share certain characteristics.

perissodactyl—a hoofed mammal with an odd number of toes.

phylum (plural phyla)—a group of creatures within a kingdom that share certain characteristics.

poacher—someone who illegally traps or kills animals.

predator—an animal that hunts and eats other animals.

species—a group of creatures within a genus that share certain characteristics. Members of the same species can mate and produce healthy young.

stallion—a male horse, ass, or zebra.

territory—the area an animal claims as its own. An animal hunts, sleeps, mates, and raises young within its territory.

ungulate—a mammal with hooves.

Learning More

Books

Adelman, Elizabeth Fagan and Wills, Jan. *Rand McNally Children's Atlas of World Wildlife*. New York: Rand McNally, 1990.

Gobble, Kelvin. *Wildlife in the Savanna*. Los Angeles: Price Stern Sloan, 1995.

Jauck, Andreas and Points, Larry. *Assateague: Island of the Wild Ponies*. New York: MacMillan, 1993.

Maynard, Thane. *A Rhino Comes to America*. Chicago: Franklin Watts, 1993.

Videos

The Rhino War. National Geographic Video.

Zebra: Patterns in the Grass. National Geographic Video.

Web Sites

Rhino Links

http://www.planetpets.simplenet.com/rhinolink.htm

A list of links sites with information about rhinos.

KBR Wild Horse and Burro

http://www.ecis.com/~whl/pag/blmhorse.html

Contains information about wild horses and burros, and tells you where you can see these animals in the United States and other parts of the world.

The Tapir Gallery

http://www.tapirback.com/tapirgal/default.htm

Pictures and basic information about tapirs and tapir conservation.

Index

About the Author

Sara Swan Miller has enjoyed working with children all her life, first as a Montessori nursery-school teacher, and later as an outdoor environmental educator at the Mohonk Preserve in New Paltz, New York. As the director of the Preserve school program, she has led hundreds of children on field trips and taught them the importance of appreciating and respecting the natural world.

She has written a number of children's books, including *Three Stories You Can Read to Your Dog*; *Three Stories You Can Read to Your Cat*; *What's in the Woods? An Outdoor Activity Book*; *Oh, Cats of Camp Rabbitbone!*; *Piggy in the Parlor and Other Tales*; *Better Than TV*; and *Will You Sting Me? Will You Bite? The Truth About Some Scary-Looking Insects*. She has also written many other books in the Animals in Order series.

BUILDING

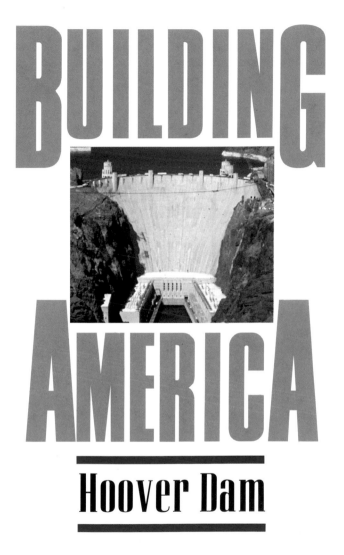

AMERICA

Hoover Dam

Craig A. Doherty and Katherine M. Doherty

A BLACKBIRCH PRESS BOOK

WOODBRIDGE, CONNECTICUT

Special Thanks

The authors wish to thank the many librarians who helped them find the research materials for this series—especially Donna Campbell, Barbara Barbieri, Yvonne Thomas, and the librarians at the New Hampshire State Library.

The publisher would like to thank Bethe Visick and Robert V. Walsh of the U.S. Department of the Interior's Bureau of Reclamation for their valuable help in completing this project.

Published by Blackbirch Press, Inc.
One Bradley Road
Woodbridge, CT 06525

© 1995 Blackbirch Press, Inc.
First Edition

Printed in Hong Kong

10 9 8 7 6 5 4 3 2 1

Photo Credits

Cover and title page: Courtesy U.S. Department of the Interior/Bureau of Reclamation.

Pages 6, 14, 16, 18, 20, 23, 27–34, 36 (top), 37–40, 42–43: courtesy U.S. Department of the Interior/Bureau of Reclamation; page 8: ©Ben Blankenburg/Leo de Wys, Inc.; page 11: U.S. Department of the Treasury; page 13: National Portrait Gallery; page 17: National Portrait Gallery; page 25: National Portrait Gallery; page 36 (bottom): ©J. Messerschmidt/Leo de Wys, Inc.

Library of Congress Cataloging-in-Publication Data

Doherty, Katherine M.
   Hoover Dam / by Katherine M. Doherty and Craig A. Doherty.—1st ed.
      p. cm.—(Building America)
  "A Blackbirch Press book."
  Includes bibliographical references and index.
  ISBN 1-56711-107-6
  1. Hoover Dam (Ariz. and Nev.)—History—Juvenile literature. 2. Colorado River (Colo.-Mexico)—Juvenile literature. [1. Hoover Dam (Ariz. and Nev.) 2. Colorado River (Colo.-Mexico)] I. Doherty, Craig A. II. Title. III. Series: Building America (Woodbridge, Conn.)
TC557.5.H6D64 1995   94-23267
627'.82—dc20   CIP
                                                AC

ACP-3834

Table of Contents

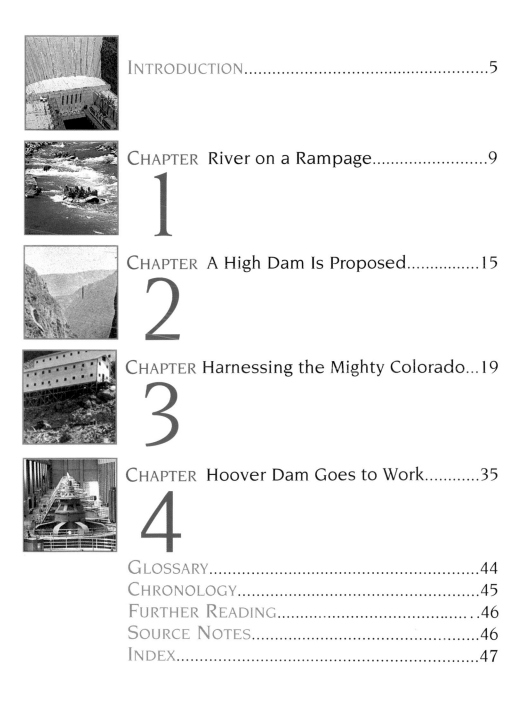

Introduction

All the brooks, streams, and rivers that drain the western slope of the Rocky Mountains from Wyoming to the Mexican border flow into the Colorado River. This mighty river carries water from parts of six states: Colorado, Arizona, Nevada, Utah, New Mexico, and Wyoming. About 741 billion cubic feet of water flow down the Colorado each year. In the past, when all the snow that fell in the mountains melted and ran down the 1,430 miles of the river, devastating floods occurred. Construction of Hoover Dam was the first step in harnessing this mighty river, and, though it solved some monumental problems, it also presented many challenges.

Before any dams were built, the Colorado was truly a wild river. Each spring it would rise and flood, while in the fall it would contain very little water. Farmers and developers in California and Arizona wanted to use the river's water to bring life to the deserts of the area, but they needed to control the river to do so. Where the river flows through Utah, northern Arizona, and southern Nevada, its channel has cut a series of deep canyons that include the magnificent Grand Canyon. Damming one of these canyons was the first logical step in taming the wild Colorado.

5

The first large-storage dam on the river was Hoover Dam. It was the largest dam in the world when it was completed in 1935. It is set in Black Canyon, on the Arizona-Nevada border, 30 miles southeast of Las Vegas, Nevada. In total, Hoover Dam stands 726.4 feet high. It is 660 feet thick at its base, and at its top it is 1,244 feet wide and 45 feet thick. The total weight of the dam is approximately 6.6 million tons. Hoover Dam was the largest government contract ever granted before World War II, and it cost $165 million to build. For all its greatness, it is considered one of the seven modern engineering wonders of the United States.

Many thousands of people were involved in the building of Hoover Dam, and millions of people have benefited from it. A number of presidents, cabinet members, governors, senators, members of the House of Representatives, and others worked out the many political problems involved in doing the project. Geologists, civil engineers, and structural engineers selected the site and designed the structure. Over 5,000 truck drivers, miners, steelworkers, cement workers, crane operators, and other construction workers did the actual work of building it. A whole new community, Boulder City, even had to be built in order to give the workers and their families a safe and clean place to live while the building took place. There was no single construction company big enough to undertake such a massive project. Before the contract was signed, six large construction companies had joined together to bid on, and eventually build, the gigantic Hoover Dam.

Starting in 1931, Hoover Dam took four-and-a-half years to build. The plans for the damming of the Colorado, however, began to take shape in 1902, with President Theodore Roosevelt. President Roosevelt signed the Reclamation Act that started a series of studies and reports on controlling the river that, eventually, led to the construction of one of the world's largest and most important dams.

An aerial view of Boulder City, a town that was created to house the many workers that played a part in building Hoover Dam.

River on a Rampage

After the Colorado River flows through a series of canyons, it enters one of the hottest and driest areas of the United States. Here, where the river forms the border between Arizona and California, summertime temperatures often exceed 100 degrees Fahrenheit. It's not unusual for the temperature to reach 125 degrees. Back in the early 1900s, many people felt that this desert area could be used for farming if the waters of the Colorado could be harnessed for irrigation. A canal, completed in 1901, began on the river only 100 yards north of the spot where the Colorado enters the country of Mexico. It proceeded south and west into Mexico

Opposite:
Rafters take on the waters of the mighty Colorado, one of America's largest and most powerful rivers.

9

before turning north and delivering water to the Imperial Valley of California.

The Imperial Valley, a huge basin located in the California desert, starts out 100 feet above sea level at its rim and drops to approximately 230 feet below sea level. The bottom of the valley, known as the Salton Sink, was the site of an ancient lake that had evaporated over thousands of years as the hot climate of the Southwest became drier. When the canal was completed, farmers rushed to the area, where they could buy land for $1.25 an acre. By 1904, about 7,000 people had moved to the valley to work the land, and agricultural production was better than expected. The developers and the farmers they attracted to the area, however, did not understand the power and the dangers of the wild river nearby.

The canal was already beginning to fill in with sediment from the river when a series of floods, from March through November 1905, wiped out the control gates. Soon, the entire Colorado River was flowing into the Imperial Valley. For the people living in the valley, it was a major disaster: Homes were lost, farmland was flooded, and the railroad had to move its tracks to higher ground. In the year it took to get the river back on its original course, a 65-foot-deep, 30-mile-long, and 10-mile-wide lake—named the Salton Sea—was created.

Before people could solve the problems created by the first flood, the river once again went on a rampage. On December 5, 1906, floodwater flowed into the Colorado from the Gila River, and, once again, the river changed its course and flowed into the Salton Sea. The lessons learned during the first floods, however, had taught people how to work with the river. By February 10, 1907, the Colorado was once more flowing into Mexico. Over the next ten years, battles raged between the river and the desert's inhabitants who wanted to use its water. Most of the time, however, the river won.

Fighting the Political Battles

As a result of President Theodore Roosevelt's initiative in 1902, Arthur Powell Davis, the director of the U.S. Reclamation Service, studied and explored the possibilities of harnessing the Colorado. His uncle, John Wesley Powell, had been the first person to

In 1902, during the administration of Theodore Roosevelt, the idea of harnessing the Colorado River for irrigation and power started to become a reality.

navigate the river through its entire course. It was partly for this reason that Davis had a special interest in the Colorado. When, in 1919, a group of Californians sent a plan to Congress for the All-American Canal to irrigate the Imperial Valley once again, Davis was instrumental in stopping the bill. He felt that the irrigation project for the valley needed to be part of a much larger project to harness the water in the entire seven-state drainage area.

Congress agreed with Davis and directed the Interior Department to study the area and report back to it. A team of hydrologists—scientists who study water and its effects—and geologists studied the river, while the politicians dealt with the sticky issue of water rights. In 1921, President Warren G. Harding appointed his secretary of commerce, Herbert Hoover, to represent the federal government on a commission to deal with the water rights issues of the Colorado drainage. Working with representatives from the seven states, Hoover ironed out an agreement, known as the Colorado River Compact, that was signed on November 24, 1922, in Santa Fe, New Mexico.

While Secretary Hoover dealt with water rights, the engineers, geologists, and other members of the surveying crews were on the river and in the canyons. During the 1920s, and even today, most of the Colorado River basin was a wilderness. The survey parties had no choice but to camp out. After gathering extensive information about the river and the lands surrounding it, a report—referred to as the Fall-Davis Report—was finally submitted to the U.S. Congress in 1922.

WATER RIGHTS AND THE HOOVER COMPROMISE

In the United States, two types of water rights are recognized by the courts: riparian rights and prior appropriation. Riparian rights state that anyone living along a waterway has the right to use water that lies within, or flows through, the boundaries of their property. The other system of water usage is known as prior appropriation rights. Under this law, the first people to legally use the water have priority. Of the seven states involved in the water rights debate for the dam, only California still recognized riparian rights.

Herbert Hoover

When the Colorado River Commission was formed in 1921 to deal with water rights, the secretary of commerce, Herbert Hoover, was elected to chair the group. Hoover quickly realized that he was faced with a number of problems between the states. For one, they could not agree on a way to divide up the water of the river. Hoover proposed a compromise that divided the drainage into upper and lower halves. The dividing point would be a place on the river called Lee Ferry, in Arizona, 30 miles south of the Utah-Arizona border. New Mexico, Wyoming, Colorado, and Utah were included as upper basin states. Nevada, Arizona, and California were considered lower basin states.

The states all thought this was a very good idea and agreed to the first part of the Hoover Compromise. The second part of the plan left the actual plan for sharing the water to be settled by the states at a later time. The states also believed that this was a good idea. Hoover's Compromise led to the signing of the Colorado River Compact by all members of the commission in Santa Fe, New Mexico, on November 24, 1922.

Although Hoover's Compromise cleared the way for the dam that would eventually be named for him, it was not until 1964 that the issue of how much water each state would get was settled. The upper basin states had reached agreement on their shares of the water by signing the 1948 Upper Colorado River Basin Compact. The lower basin states, however, couldn't reach agreement. In 1952, their case went to the U.S. Supreme Court, and the Court appointed a Special Master to listen to all sides of the argument. Over the next eight years, the Special Master heard from state and local governments, companies, and many private individuals—everyone who had a stake in the water of the river had a chance to state their case.

The Special Master gave his recommendations to the Court in 1960, and the Supreme Court handed down its decision during its 1964 session. The Court said that California was to get 4.4 million acre-feet of water, Nevada was to get 300,000 acre-feet, and Arizona was to get 2.8 million acre-feet. An acre-foot is the quantity of water it would take to cover an acre of land one foot deep, which is about 326,000 gallons.

A High Dam Is Proposed

The Fall-Davis Report (Albert B. Fall was the secretary of the interior, Arthur P. Davis was director of the Reclamation Service, a branch of the Interior Department) proposed that the U.S. government build a high dam "at or near Boulder Canyon." The report went on to say that the government would eventually get back the money it spent on the dam by selling the electricity that the dam would generate. If Congress approved the plan, many of the problems of the lower river would be solved.

The report gave Congress detailed information about the river and the land through which it passes. In 1928, armed with the information from the Fall-Davis Report, Congress passed the Boulder Canyon Project Act, which provided for the financing of a high dam at or near Boulder Canyon.

Opposite:
Workers explore the Black Canyon dam site in 1922, almost ten years before any work began.

15

Which Canyon to Dam and How to Dam It

At first, the dam was to be built at Boulder Canyon, and it was referred to as Boulder Dam. Black Canyon, 20 miles downstream from Boulder Canyon and 30 miles southeast of Las Vegas, Nevada, however, turned out to be the better site. A reservoir of equal capacity would be created behind the Black Canyon site, and the dam would not have to be as high as at Boulder. There was, however, controversy surrounding the decision. Some of the geologists felt that the Boulder site would be better because the underlying rock there was granite, while the foundations of Black Canyon were volcanic rock. In the end, after Congress had called in independent engineers to study the situation, it was decided that Black Canyon would be the right place for the dam.

With the site selected, the engineers in the Bureau of Reclamation's Denver office proceeded to design what would be the world's tallest dam. Dozens of engineers worked on the project, combining their years of experience building dams with the difficult demands of harnessing the West's most powerful river.

The design they came up with called for a dam that would stand over 725 feet tall and 1,244 feet across at the top. The base of the dam would be 660 feet thick, and it would taper to just 45 feet

An engineer's sketch shows how the various outlets and spillways of the dam would work.

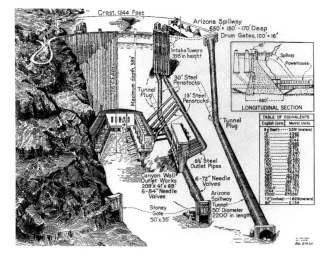

BOULDER DAM OR HOOVER DAM?

In 1928, during Calvin Coolidge's presidency, the U. S. Congress passed the Boulder Canyon Project Act, which provided the Interior Department with the authority and financing to build a dam "at or near Boulder Canyon." Although the dam had no official name at this time, it was popularly referred to as Boulder Dam. On September 17, 1930, President Hoover's secretary of the interior, Ray L. Wilbur, attended a special spike-driving ceremony for the railway that would go to Black Canyon, where the dam was soon to be built. At this ceremony, Wilbur surprised the assembled engineers, government workers, reporters, and others by stating the dam would be called Hoover Dam in

Calvin Coolidge approved the Boulder Canyon Project Act.

honor of the current president.

The media was stunned, and wrote many negative statements about this sudden and unannounced name change. On May 8, 1933, after Franklin D. Roosevelt became president and Harold L. Ickes became his secretary of the interior, Secretary Ickes changed the name of the dam officially to Boulder Dam. It seemed to many that the newly elected democratic president and his advisors did not want to have to finish a dam named for their Republican predecessor. Hoover, however, felt insulted by the name change. In 1947, a joint resolution of the Congress wiped away that insult by changing the name back to Hoover Dam, the name it has kept to this day.

at the top. The design they created is called a concrete thick-arch dam, which uses the arched shape to transfer to the walls of the canyon the stresses of holding back the water. Tunnels would also be dug through the canyon walls, and structures would be built at the base of the dam to house the power plants.

In 1929, the final design for the dam was approved by the Colorado River Board. This was an agency set up by Congress to oversee the planning and construction of the dam. With an approved design, companies could now bid on the project and then start construction.

Harnessing the Mighty Colorado

The dam to be built at Black Canyon was such a massive project that no one company was big enough to do it. Six of the country's largest construction companies— Utah Construction Co., J.F. Shea Co., Morrison-Knudsen Co., MacDonald and Kahn Co., Henry J. Kaiser and W.A. Bechtel Co., and Pacific Bridge Co.—officially joined together to become Six Companies, Incorporated, and bid on the project. On March 11, 1931, Ray L. Wilbur, secretary of the interior, awarded the contract to Six Companies, whose bid of $48,890,995.50 was the lowest of all those submitted. With the largest single contract ever signed by the U.S. government at that time, construction on the great dam could now begin.

Opposite:
The first bunkhouses for workers from Six Companies appeared in Black Canyon around 1931.

R.F. Walter (seated) signed the contract with Six Companies in April 1931. The bid submitted promised that the project would be completed for less than $49 million.

The man who was appointed to oversee the construction of the dam was Frank T. Crowe, the chief engineer for Morrison-Knudsen Co. and the most respected dam builder in the country. Before Crowe and the thousands of workers from Six Companies could get started, however, there were many problems that had to be solved. Among them, railroads had to be built, housing and services for the workers were needed, and the wild and powerful water of the mighty Colorado had to be diverted.

Getting There

The site chosen for Hoover Dam was 30 miles from Las Vegas, Nevada, the nearest town. There was no easy way to get the workers and supplies to Black Canyon. The engineers who had been working at the site had been camping out, and the first workers who arrived in the area did the same. The campsites took on colorful names, such as Ragtown. They were not, however, colorful places to live. It was hot in the canyon; the average daily high during July 1931, was 119 degrees Fahrenheit. The average low was 95. There was no electricity at the campsites and very little in the way of sanitation. The drinking water soon became contaminated with bacteria, which caused many of the workers and their families to get a serious disease called amoebic dysentery.

To address some of the problems of the campsites, a road, a railroad, and power lines were built to Black Canyon. As soon as Six Companies could get equipment and materials to the site, housing was built for the workers. Engineers from the Bureau of Reclamation selected a site seven miles southwest of Black Canyon for the housing project. By the time they were done, a completely new town, Boulder City, Nevada, had been created. Boulder City provided new houses for the workers to rent, and it also had schools, stores, churches, parks, and paved streets. Once the workers were living in Boulder City, the problems with the heat and sanitation were greatly lessened.

Four Tunnels for the Colorado

Before construction could begin on the actual dam, the waters of the Colorado had to be diverted, or rechanneled. Because of the narrowness of Black Canyon, there was only one way to divert the river: that was to send it through tunnels in the canyon walls. The engineers designed the tunnels so that they would be used later in the operation of the dam. Two inner tunnels on each side of the canyon would be used to bring water to, and take water from, the huge generators that would be installed in the base of the dam. Outer tunnels would also be incorporated into spillways designed to carry any overflow during the periods of heavy flooding. Excavation of the four tunnels started in June 1931, and by November 14, 1932, the water of the mighty Colorado ran through the first two tunnels, which had been completed on the Arizona side of the river.

When they were finished, the four tunnels had a combined length of just over three miles. It took over 3.5 million pounds of dynamite to blast the 56-foot-diameter holes through the solid rock. More than 1.5 million cubic yards of rock were removed from the tunnels and dumped in a nearby canyon. After the tunnels were dug out, they were lined with a three-foot-thick layer of concrete. The concrete reinforced the rock wall and smoothed its surface, allowing the water to flow through with greater ease.

Digging the tunnels was one of the most danger-ous aspects of the entire Hoover Dam project. Six Companies had a very short deadline to get the river diverted, and if they missed their deadline they would have to pay a $3,000-per-day penalty. In the tunnels, safety was often sacrificed for speed. The procedure for digging the diversions involved drilling, blasting, removing the loosened rock, and then repeating the process. Ten to 20 feet of rock would be drilled and blasted at a time. With crews working around the clock in all four tunnels at the same time, up to 250 feet of tunnel would be dug in

a day. Temperatures inside the tunnels often rose to 140 degrees Fahrenheit, and between June 25, and July 26, 1931, there were 14 workers who died from the heat in the canyon.

Despite the grueling work conditions, hard-rock miners from all over the West came to work on the tunnels. Many of these men were of Irish descent and were experts at what they did. But even with experienced miners doing the work, accidents

Workers from Six Companies stand upon a special drill rig that was mounted on a truck. The rig was used in the construction of the diversion tunnels.

Franklin Delano Roosevelt Saves a Dam

In 1902, President Theodore Roosevelt put his signature on the Reclamation Act and started the U.S. government down the road that would eventually lead to the construction of Hoover Dam. Presidents Coolidge, Harding, and Hoover got the project started, but it was left to President Franklin Delano Roosevelt (FDR) to see that the project was finished. When FDR took office in January 1933, the construction of Hoover Dam was well underway, but the economy of the country was in a shambles. Many people in Congress and elsewhere thought the government could not continue to afford such an expensive construction project.

FDR and his advisors saw the situation quite differently. While campaigning for the presidency, FDR had promised a "New Deal" for the American people. This New Deal would provide reform of the social welfare system and attempt to stimulate economic recovery for the entire country. Federal agencies, such as the Civilian Conservation Corps (CCC), the Works Project Administration (WPA), the Federal Housing Administration (FHA), and the National Recovery Administration (NRA), were formed to bring the programs of the New Deal to the people.

Franklin Delano Roosevelt

Hoover Dam was seen by FDR as an example of how a large-scale public project could help the economy of an area, and put thousands of people back to work. When Congress voted to leave the funding for the continuation of Boulder Canyon Project out of their budget, FDR reinstated it. Without FDR's foresight and understanding of the economic situation, Hoover Dam might never have been completed.

happened. The tunnels themselves were dangerous places because of the heat, potential for collapse, and, also, because of the toxic carbon monoxide fumes from vehicles and equipment working in them.

As if the human-made dangers weren't enough, mother nature made the situation even more risky for the workers. In the early days of February 1932, rain in the mountains of Utah sent floodwaters down the Colorado. On February 9, the water rose an astonishing 11 feet in 12 hours. The work in the canyon came to a halt as men and equipment were moved to higher ground. The river rose again the next day and, on February 12, came up 17 feet in three hours. The rush of water washed away the tunnel's protective levees and caused the unfinished tunnels to flood. It took crews a week to repair the levees and clean up the mud that the torrents had left behind.

Despite the human-made dangers and the added natural disasters, the tunnels were completed on time. Cofferdams—temporary dams that hold water away from a work area—were built to send the river into the tunnels, and to keep the water from flowing back upstream to the dam site. With the river successfully diverted, Six Companies could now start work on the main structure of the dam.

Getting Down to Bedrock

The diversion of the river gave the workers about one mile of dry riverbed in which to work. Here, they would build the 660-foot-thick base of the dam, as well as the housing for the power generators. Before they could start building, however, huge

A Spiderweb of Cables

Workers ride a skip on one of the cableways.

These cables were strung between two 90-foot-high towers, one on each side of the canyon. The towers were set on tracks so they could move. A carriage, containing pulleys and cables to move objects up and down, was attached to the main cables. The carriage could be moved in and out while the towers could be moved back and forth. This allowed the cableway operator to lower a load to the exact spot where it was needed below.

Being the cableway operator was a very demanding job. The operator worked the controls from a small building that was on a platform built 30 feet out over the canyon. Today, crane operators communicate with the workers over radios. At this time, however, the operator had to depend on hand and arm signals and a series of electrically operated bells to know when and where to lower objects.

The primary use of the cableway was raising and lowering the huge concrete buckets. People and materials also went up and down with the cableway. When workers needed to go up or down from the job site they would ride in a "skip." A skip was a railed wooden platform that could hold up to 50 workers a trip. If the cable was twisted, the skip would

Although roads were built down into the canyon, it was a slow and inefficient method of moving people and materials. Fortunately, Frank T. Crowe, the chief engineer and superintendent of construction on the project, had special skills in designing and using cableways. A cableway is a series of cables strung, in this case across the top of the canyon, and used for lowering and raising workers and materials to and from the work site.

The main cableway used at Hoover Dam consisted of five primary cables, each rated for a 20-ton load.

spin on the way down. A skiptender rode down with the workers and was responsible for signalling to the operator. Sometimes, if the wrong signal was given, the skip would stop in mid-air. On January 1, 1933, a serious disaster was narrowly avoided when a skip crashed into the canyon wall on the Arizona side. All of the passengers were knocked from their feet, but no one fell off. Other men were not as lucky. Two men died as a result of cableway accidents. One accident was on January 3, 1935, when the hoist line broke on a bucket of concrete and a man was thrown 150 feet. Another man was killed by a broken cable on February 19, 1935.

Although the cableway was the best way to get heavy loads of materials in and out of the canyon, the workers also used another device to get to and from their work site. These devices were called "monkey slides" and were like a vertical railroad.

The canyon wall, and later the face of the dam, had a set of tracks attached. Up to 50 men could ride on special platforms up or down the tracks. The platform rode on greased skids and was lowered down and pulled up on a cable by a 75 horsepower winch that wound the cable around a giant spool.

The cableway enabled large pieces of equipment and parts to be put easily into position. (Note the worker riding in the piece of tunnel pipe.)

power shovels were needed to remove over half-a-million cubic yards of mud and muck from the riverbed. A dam of this size needed to rest on solid bedrock.

As in other aspects of the construction, speed was very important to the builders. During this phase of construction, a competition was held between the three shifts to see which crew could move the most material out of the riverbed. The swing shift—the shift between the day shift and the night shift—won when it moved a total of 1,841 truckloads of river bottom on January 24, 1933. The crews finally hit bedrock 40 feet down in the riverbed.

Once they had cleared down to the bedrock, workers found a number of springs coming up through the rock. A network of drainpipes had to be put in to remove the water, and the springs needed to be sealed off so the water would not interfere with the base of the dam.

Hanging from a Rope

While the crews worked around the clock to prepare the riverbed for construction, the sides of the canyon had to be shaped so they would join smoothly with the dam. This was the job of workers called "high scalers," who hung from ropes and cables anchored into the sides of the canyon. It took the high scalers four months and 185 tons of dynamite to remove almost 1 million cubic yards of rock from the canyon walls. High scalers included people who had worked as sailors or circus performers, and six Apaches from the area. No matter what their previous experience, these daredevils had to be both fearless and in top

physical condition. This was the most dangerous job on the entire project, and the high scalers were paid accordingly. They took home $5.60 per day—forty percent more than the men who worked in the tunnels.

One of the worst dangers for these workers was rock and other debris falling on them. Many high scalers made crude hard hats by dipping cloth hats in tar and leaving them out in the hot desert sun to

High scalers suspended by cables worked to remove loosened rock and to smooth the rough surface of the canyon walls.

Even though the high scalers were attached to ropes for safety, their job was the most dangerous of the entire project. Here, high scalers drill into the canyon rock more than 500 feet above the Colorado River.

dry. After a few men were saved from injury by their homemade hard hats, Six Companies ordered thousands of commercially made hard hats and suggested that everyone wear one.

A Mountain of Concrete

On June 6, 1933, the first bucket of concrete was poured into the base of Hoover Dam. But pouring the concrete created a number of problems for the engineers. The chemical reaction that takes place as cement hardens creates heat. The engineers figured that, if the dam was poured as one solid block, it would take 125 years to cool down and would crack, becoming useless.

To prevent these problems with the concrete, the engineers made two decisions: First, they poured the concrete in small blocks, with each block being between 25 and 60 feet square and 5 feet thick. It took 230 squares to make up the base of the dam. Second, in each square, they installed a gridwork of one-inch-steel pipe through which they ran cold water. This sped up the cooling process and allowed the workers the opportunity to fill the cracks and joints caused by the contracting concrete. In all, 582 miles of water pipe were laid in the dam. Thanks to

The dam, under construction in 1933. The concrete was poured in a series of blocks so that each block could be cooled before new concrete was added.

By 1934, the outlets for two of the diversion tunnels were complete and the dam had nearly reached its finished height.

the creative problem solving of the engineers, the concrete was cool enough by March of 1935, rather than in 2058 (which is when the dam would have finally cooled if it had been left alone).

Prior to 1933, the Bureau of Reclamation had used a total of 5.8 million barrels of cement in all the dams it had built up to that time. The Hoover Dam project alone used more than 5 million barrels of cement. Every day during the pouring of the dam, workers would use between 25 and 35 railroad-car loads of cement. When mixed with sand, water, and aggregate (crushed rock), almost 4.4 million yards of concrete were eventually put into the dam. The same amount of concrete could pave a 16-foot-wide highway from Los Angeles to Boston!

As the concrete was poured into the forms, it was the job of workers known as "puddlers" to spread and pack it. Up to 1,100 buckets a day were lowered into the canyon, where the puddlers used their feet and shovels to work the concrete. Although there were many rumors at the time about workers getting buried alive in the grey muck, only one man died while pouring concrete and his body was recovered. The last of the concrete was finally added to the dam on February 6, 1935.

Looking at the dam from the "back" (downstream view) in January 1935, the four nearly completed intake towers could be seen.

About the same time, the gates on the diversion tunnels were closed and newly formed Lake Mead began to fill. Construction crews continued to work on the buildings for the power generators and other final elements. The government had allowed Six Companies seven years to build what was, at the time, the world's largest dam, but it had only taken them five years to complete the project. Some have compared this feat to building the great pyramids in Egypt, which took 100,000 workers 20 years to finish.

Hoover Dam
Goes to Work

On September 30, 1935, more than 12,000 people joined President Franklin Delano Roosevelt at the dam, and many more listened on the radio, as he made a speech dedicating the gigantic new structure. His voice echoing through the canyon over an amplified sound system, Roosevelt announced:

> This is an engineering victory of the first order—another great achievement of American resourcefulness, skill, and determination. This is why I have the right once more to congratulate you who have created Boulder Dam and on behalf of the nation to say to you, 'well done.'

Opposite: Seventeen massive generators inside, at the base of the dam, generate nearly 3 million horsepower. The electricity they produce provides power to three states.

35

The U-shaped structure at the base of the dam houses the generators.

Although the dam had been dedicated by the president, the work was not quite done. Nearly 500 workers still labored at the site, installing the first of the generators and doing other last-minute work.

The Power Factor

The electric generators at Hoover Dam are located in a U-shaped building at the base of the structure. Today, there are 17 huge generators in operation, combining to generate a total of nearly 3 million horsepower. The powerhouse is divided into two wings, which are referred to as the Nevada and Arizona wings. There are approximately ten acres of floor space in the powerhouse, and the water is brought down to the generators through a complex system of tunnels and pipes. The water enters the power system from the four intake towers that stand behind the dam, two on each side. The towers are almost 400 feet tall and have an inside diameter of 82 feet at their base. The electricity generated by Hoover Dam provides power to Arizona, Nevada, and southern California over a vast network of high-voltage power lines. Hoover Dam has also helped the region grow safely by providing a stable, clean, and inexpensive source of electricity. It would take an estimated 8 million barrels of oil a year to generate the electricity provided by the dam.

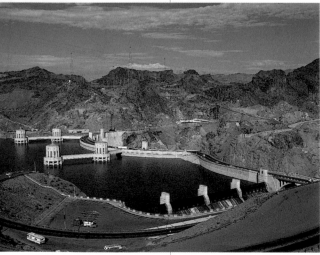

Four intake towers at the top of the dam help to bring water to the generators.

The Desert Blooms

The All-American Canal that was built as part of the Boulder Canyon Project Act brings irrigation water to approximately 500,000 acres in California's Imperial Valley. Another canal was built to bring water to the Coachella Valley, which is on the northern shore of the Salton Sea in California, and has the capacity to irrigate another 78,500 acres. The Yuma Project brings water from the Colorado to another 68,000 acres in Arizona and California. The irrigated lands of the area can be used for growing crops year round. Alfalfa, cotton, sugar beets, dates, citrus fruits, winter vegetables, and a variety of other crops all thrive in this area.

Lighted by its own power, Hoover Dam offers a dramatic view to visitors at night.

Lake Mead

From the time they shut the diverting gates in 1935, it took six-and-a-half years to fill Lake Mead. (Today, when a dam is built, the engineers fill the reservoirs much more slowly. They do this because rapid filling creates such great pressure on a dam and poses some possible danger of earthquakes.) The enormous weight of the water forced the land to settle, which, in turn, created small earthquakes. The worst quake measured 5.0 on the Richter Scale. The earthquakes continue to this day but are infrequent and hardly noticeable.

When full, the lake is 589 feet at its deepest point, covers 247 square miles, and has 550 miles of

Created by the completion of Hoover Dam, Lake Mead is a popular location for many kinds of water-related recreation.

shoreline. The lake is 110 miles long, running from the dam to the western end of the Grand Canyon. Lake Mead was named after Dr. Elwood Mead, who was the commissioner of the Bureau of Reclamation from 1924 to 1936. Today, the lake is operated as a national recreation area by the National Park Service.

The level of the lake varies according to the seasons. In the spring, the run-off from the mountains, which had caused devastating floods in the past, causes the water level to rise. In the fall and winter, the level of the lake may be intentionally lowered to make room for the next year's floodwaters and to maintain a constant flow to the lower river and its irrigation projects. In addition to serving its original purpose—to control the flow of the river—Lake Mead has become a popular spot for boating and fishing.

Top:
The Arizona spillway has remained dry for most of the dam's history.
Bottom:
In July 1983, water from spring and early summer floods flowed over the top of the spillway gates.

Still a Wild River

In 1983, the Colorado proved that, although harnessed by its dams, it had not been entirely tamed. The regulations set by the U.S. Corps of Engineers make sure that there is always enough space in the reservoirs of the river to contain the spring floods. Despite having more room for floodwater than required, the water in 1983 kept rising through the spring and into the early summer until, on

July 2, water started pouring over the Hoover Dam spillways. Except for testing the spillways in 1941, this was the first time water had flowed *over* the spillway gates. Water levels going over the spillways rose to four feet deep and fell at more than 100 miles per hour into the tunnels below.

Because of the dam and the spillways, the floods of 1983 were minor in comparison to those experienced in the early part of the century. Hoover Dam, and the other dams that were built above and below it, proved that the area's people were no longer totally at the mercy of the river.

12 Dams and a New Visitor Center

Starting with Morelos Dam near Yuma, Arizona, and ending with the Fontenelle Dam on the Green River in Wyoming, there are 10 other major dams in the Colorado system: Parker and Davis are on the

When completed, the new visitor center will better serve the many hundreds of thousands of tourists that arrive at Hoover Dam each year.

Colorado below Hoover Dam. Glen Canyon Dam is just above Lee Ferry, Arizona, near where the Colorado crosses the border between Utah and Arizona. The other dams are on tributaries of the Colorado. Morrow Point, Crystal, and Blue Mesa dams are on the Gunnison River in Colorado; Navajo Dam is on the San Juan in New Mexico; and the Flaming Gorge and Fontenelle dams are on the Green River in Utah and Wyoming respectively.

Some of the water from the river travels through the Colorado River Aqueduct to supply some of the drinking water for Los Angeles, California. The newest project on the river now takes water for irrigation to central Arizona. The lakes behind the dams have become great spots for fishing, boating, and other recreational activities, and they have created new wetlands for birds and other animals who could not survive on the banks of a wild river.

The Bureau of Reclamation finally has this mighty river working *for* people instead of against them, and has now turned its attention to better serving the over 750,000 tourists who come to visit Hoover Dam each year. A new visitor center is being built that, when finished, will have a cost totaling an estimated $120 million.

Hoover Dam has stood for 60 years as a monument to the abilities and ingenuity of humankind. It proves that, working together, people are capable of coming up with a solution to just about any problem, no matter what its size. In the case of Hoover Dam, the skill, hard work, and dedication of countless Americans finally made this great solution a reality.

The success of the Hoover Dam project shows the great potential of human engineering. In less than four years of construction, one of America's mightiest rivers had been tamed and its power had been harnessed to benefit millions of people.

Glossary

acre-foot The amount of water it takes to cover an acre of land one foot deep; approximately 326,000 gallons.

amoebic dysentery A disease, usually caused by bacteria in drinking water, that causes a person to have severe diarrhea. It can be fatal if the victim becomes severely dehydrated.

appropriation rights The right to use a source of water granted to the first person to use the water.

arch dam A dam in the shape of an arch that transfers the main stresses caused by the weight of the water to the rock walls against which the dam is built.

bedrock The underlying layer of solid rock.

cableway A complex device used to raise and lower people and materials to a work site.

canal A human-made waterway.

carbon monoxide An odorless and invisible gas that is the by-product of the internal combustion engine. It can be fatal if breathed in.

civil engineer An engineer who is trained to design and build public works such as roads, harbors, and dams.

cofferdam A temporary dam used to protect a work site that is below the normal level of the water.

cubic foot A measurement of volume that would fill a cube that is one foot long on all sides.

diversion The rerouting of the river.

geologist A scientist who studies the formation of the earth and the rock structure of the earth's surface.

granite A very hard igneous rock formation.

hard hat A protective helmet worn by construction workers.

high scaler The workers who hung by ropes and prepared the cliffs of Black Canyon to receive the sides of Hoover Dam.

intake tower The structure at a dam that takes water from the reservoir and directs it to the power-generating machinery.

irrigation Supplementing crops with additional water. Through the practices of irrigation, crops can be grown in areas that would otherwise be too dry.

levee Usually made of earth, a levee is built to protect a low lying area from floods.

monkey slide A device that was used to primarily move workers down to and up from the work site in the bottom of the canyon.

powerhouse The building used to house the power-generating machinery. A powerhouse is usually found at the downstream base of a dam.

pulley A wheel or series of wheels with ropes or cables wrapped around them used to give a mechanical advantage when lifting a heavy object.

riparian rights Water rights that state that the owner of a property has a right to water that passes through or is adjacent to their property.

sediment The particles of soil carried by the river water. Sediment created many problems during the early attempts to use the water of the Colorado.

skip A large platform with a railing around it that would be raised and lowered to the bottom of the canyon by the cableway and was one of the ways workers got to and from the job site.

skip tender The person on the skip who would direct the cableway operator as to where and when to raise and lower the skip.

Special Master The person appointed by the U.S. Supreme Court to gather information about the dispute between California, Arizona, and Nevada over the appropriation of the water from the Colorado River. The Supreme Court finally settled the dispute in 1964.

structural engineer An engineer who is trained in the materials and stresses involved in building structures.

volcanic rock Rock that was created by a volcano.

winch A mechanical device used to wind up a cable or rope. Small winches are operated by hand, while large winches are operated by motors.

CHRONOLOGY

1905 Imperial Valley is flooded and Salton Sea is created.

1919 All-American Canal Board calls for construction of a canal and reservoirs on the Colorado River.

1920 Kinkaid Act passes in the U.S. Congress authorizing the Bureau of Reclamation to study the problems of the Colorado River drainage.

1922 Fall-Davis Report recommends construction of the All-American Canal and a high dam "at or near Boulder Canyon."

Colorado River Compact is signed on November 24, in Santa Fe, New Mexico, by the representatives of the seven states of the Colorado River drainage and the federal government.

1928 Boulder Canyon Project Act passes Congress and authorizes the funding and construction of the Boulder Canyon Project.

1930 Secretary of the Interior Ray L. Wilbur announces the official name as "Hoover Dam."

1931 Six Companies bids on and wins the contract to build Hoover Dam.

Work begins on diversion tunnels in Black Canyon.

1932 Colorado River is diverted through tunnels on November 14.

1933 First concrete is poured in the base of the dam on June 6.

Secretary of the Interior Harold L. Ickes changes the dam's name to "Boulder Dam."

1935 Dam starts impounding water on February 1.

Last concrete placed on dam on May 29.

President Franklin D. Roosevelt officially dedicates the dam on September 30.

1941 Lake Mead is filled.

1947 U.S. Congress officially changes the dam's name back to "Hoover Dam."

1964 U.S. Supreme Court settles water claims case between lower Colorado basin states.

1983 First uncontrolled discharge of water from Lake Mead.

1991 New visitor center construction begins.

FURTHER READING

Ardley, Neil. *Dams*. Ada, OK: Garrett Educational, 1990.

Ayer, Eleanor. *Our Great Rivers and Waterways*. Brookfield, CT: Millbrook Press, 1994.

Boring, Mel. *Incredible Constructions and the People Who Built Them*. New York: Walker & Co., 1985.

Clinton, Susan. *Herbert Hoover*. Chicago: Childrens Press, 1988.

Dunn, Andrew. *Dams*. New York: Thomson Learning, 1993.

Morgan, Sally and Morgan, Adrian. *Structures*. New York: Facts On File, 1993.

Twist, Clint. *Wind & Water Power*. Chicago: Watts, 1993.

SOURCE NOTES

Hoover Dam. Washington, D.C.: GPO, 1985.

Moeller, Beverley Bowen. *Phil Swing and Boulder Dam*. Berkeley: University of California Press, 1971.

Petroski, Henry. "Hoover Dam." *American Scientist*, v 81, November-December 1981, 517-521.

Rhodes, Benjamin D. "Designing the Hoover Dam." *Essays in Colorado History*, n 10, 1989, 51-79.

"Visitor Center is a Tough Act." ENR, April 11, 1994, 24-30.

Steinberg, Theodore. "That World's Fair Feeling: Control of Water in the 20th Century." *Technology and Culture*, v 34 no 2, April 1993, 401-9.

Stevens, Joseph E. *Hoover Dam: An American Adventure*. Norman, OK: University of Oklahoma Press, 1988.

The Story of Hoover Dam. Washington, D.C.: U.S. Department of the Interior, 1961.

Wilbur, Ray Lyman and Ely, Northcutt. *The Hoover Dam Documents*. Second edition. Washington, D.C.: GPO, 1948.

INDEX